Bright Layettes to Crochet

Oh, Baby! One look at these colorful layettes and your little one's eyes will dance with joy. Besides being crocheted of soft and washable yarn, the sweet sets are also terrifically textured—perfect for tiny fingers to explore. Each outfit includes an afghan, a hat, a jacket, and a pair of booties in size six months. No time to create an entire ensemble? Then fashion your favorite afghan in a flash. A wee someone will love the warmth, and you'll love how all of these vivid designs make every day special!

LEISURE ARTS, INC.
Little Rock, Arkansas

Purple Layette

Shown on page 3.

INTERMEDIATE

Finished Size: 6 months
Chest Measurement: 17" (43 cm)
Finished Chest Measurement:
21 1/2" (54.5 cm)
Afghan: 36" x 45" (91.5 cm x 114.5 cm)

MATERIALS

Sacque, Bonnet, Booties

Sport Weight Yarn (LIGHT 3)

Complete Set

Purple - 800 yards (732 meters)

Sacque

Purple - 575 yards (526 meters)

Bonnet

Purple - 125 yards (114 meters)

Booties

Purple - 100 yards (91meters)

Crochet hooks, sizes F (3.75 mm), G (4 mm) **and** H (5 mm) **or** sizes needed for gauge
3/8" (10 mm) wide Ribbon - 3 yards (2.5 meters)
Sewing needle and thread
Yarn needle

Afghan

Medium Weight Yarn (MEDIUM 4)
[4 ounces, 242 yards (113 grams, 221 meters) per skein]:
Variegated - 10 skeins
Crochet hook, size K(6.5 mm) **or** size needed for gauge

GAUGES:

Sport Weight Yarn: 9 sts and 8 rows = 2" (5 cm)
Medium Weight Yarn (holding 2 strands of yarn together)**:** 8 sts and 7 rows = 3" (7.5 cm)

GAUGE SWATCHES:

Sport Weight Yarn: 4 1/4" x 4" (10.75 cm x 10 cm)

Using largest size hook for Sport Weight yarn and Purple, ch 20.
Row 1: Sc in second ch from hook and in each ch across: 19 sc.

Row 2-16: Work same as Rows 2-16 of Sacque Body, page 4.
Finish off.

Medium Weight Yarn: 4 1/2" (11.5 cm) square
Note: Swatch is worked holding two strands of yarn together.

Using largest size hook and Variegated, ch 10.
Rows 1-12: Work same as Afghan, page 7: 9 sts.
Finish off.

STITCH GUIDE

DECREASE (uses next 2 sts)
Pull up a loop in next 2 sts, YO and draw through all 3 loops on hook ***(counts as one sc)***.

PICOT
Ch 2, slip st in second ch from hook.

CROSS STITCH ***(abbreviated Cross St)***
Working in Back Loops Only ***(Fig. 3, page 27)***, skip next st, dc in next st, working in **front** of dc just made ***(Fig. 1)***, dc in skipped st.

Fig. 1

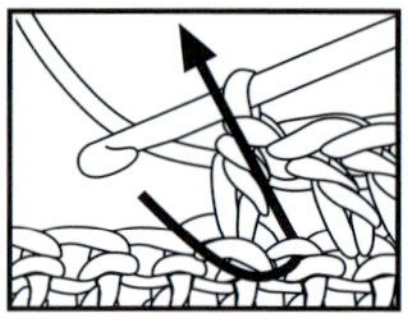

SACQUE

YOKE

With Purple and using medium size hook, ch 64.
Row 1 (Right side)**:** Sc in second ch from hook and in each ch across: 63 sc.

Note 1: Loop a short piece of yarn around any stitch to mark Row 1 as **right** side.

Instructions continued on page 4.

Work in Back Loops Only ***(Fig. 3, page 27)***, unless otherwise instructed.

Row 2: Ch 1, turn; sc in first 9 sc, 3 sc in next sc, sc in next 11 sc, 3 sc in next sc, sc in next 19 sc, 3 sc in next sc, sc in next 11 sc, 3 sc in next sc, sc in last 9 sc: 71 sc.
Row 3: Ch 1, turn; sc in first 10 sc, 3 sc in next sc, sc in next 13 sc, 3 sc in next sc, sc in next 21 sc, 3 sc in sc, sc in next 13 sc, 3 sc in next sc, sc in last 10 sc: 79 sc.
Row 4: Ch 1, turn; sc in first 11 sc, 3 sc in next sc, sc in next 15 sc, 3 sc in next sc, sc in next 23 sc, 3 sc in next sc, sc in next 15 sc, 3 sc in next sc, sc in last 11 sc: 87 sc.
Row 5: Ch 1, turn; sc in first 12 sc, 3 sc in next sc, sc in next 17 sc, 3 sc in next sc, sc in next 25 sc, 3 sc in next sc, sc in next 17 sc, 3 sc in next sc, sc in last 12 sc: 95 sc.
Row 6: Ch 1, turn; sc in first 13 sc, 3 sc in next sc, sc in next 19 sc, 3 sc in next sc, sc in next 27 sc, 3 sc in next sc, sc in next 19 sc, 3 sc in next sc, sc in last 13 sc: 103 sc.
Row 7: Ch 1, turn; sc in first 14 sc, 3 sc in next sc, sc in next 21 sc, 3 sc in next sc, sc in next 29 sc, 3 sc in next sc, sc in next 21 sc, 3 sc in next sc, sc in last 14 sc: 111 sc.
Row 8: Ch 1, turn; sc in first 15 sc, 3 sc in next sc, sc in next 23 sc, 3 sc in next sc, sc in next 31 sc, 3 sc in next sc, sc in next 23 sc, 3 sc in next sc, sc in last 15 sc: 119 sc.
Row 9: Ch 1, turn; sc in first 16 sc, 3 sc in next sc, sc in next 25 sc, 3 sc in next sc, sc in next 33 sc, 3 sc in next sc, sc in next 25 sc, 3 sc in next sc, sc in last 16 sc: 127 sc.
Row 10: Ch 1, turn; sc in first 17 sc, 3 sc in next sc, sc in next 27 sc, 3 sc in next sc, sc in next 35 sc, 3 sc in next sc, sc in next 27 sc, 3 sc in next sc, sc in last 17 sc: 135 sc.
Row 11: Ch 1, turn; sc in first 18 sc, 3 sc in next sc, sc in next 29 sc, 3 sc in next sc, sc in next 37 sc, 3 sc in next sc, sc in next 29 sc, 3 sc in next sc, sc in last 18 sc: 143 sc.
Row 12: Ch 1, turn; sc in first 19 sc, 3 sc in next sc, sc in next 31 sc, 3 sc in next sc, sc in next 39 sc, 3 sc in next sc, sc in next 31 sc, 3 sc in next sc, sc in last 19 sc: 151 sc.
Row 13: Ch 1, turn; sc in first 20 sc, 3 sc in next sc, sc in next 33 sc, 3 sc in next sc, sc in next 41 sc, 3 sc in next sc, sc in next 33 sc, 3 sc in next sc, sc in last 20 sc: 159 sc.
Row 14: Ch 1, turn; sc in first 21 sc, 3 sc in next sc, sc in next 35 sc, 3 sc in next sc, sc in next 43 sc, 3 sc in next sc, sc in next 35 sc, 3 sc in next sc, sc in last 21 sc: 167 sc; do **not** finish off.

BODY

Row 1: Ch 1, turn; sc in first 23 sc, skip next 37 sc (Sleeve), sc in next 47 sc, skip next 37 sc (Sleeve), sc in last 23 sc: 93 sc.

Change to largest size hook for Sport Weight yarn.

Row 2: Ch 3 ***(counts as first dc, now and throughout)***, turn; work Cross St across ***(Fig. 1, page 2)***: 93 dc.
Rows 3-5: Ch 1, turn; sc in each st across.
Rows 6-26: Repeat Rows 2-5, 5 times; then repeat Row 2 once **more**, do **not** finish off.

EDGING

Rnd 1: Ch 1, turn; working in both loops, 3 sc in first dc, work 94 sc evenly spaced across to last dc, 3 sc in last dc, work 40 sc evenly spaced across end of rows; working in free loops of beginning ch ***(Fig. 2, page 27)***, 3 sc in first ch, skip next ch, sc in next 7 chs, skip next ch, sc in next 11 chs, skip next ch, sc in next 20 chs, skip next ch, sc in next 10 chs, skip next ch, sc in next 7 chs, skip next ch, 3 sc in last ch; work 40 sc evenly spaced across end of rows; join with slip st to first sc: 241 sc.

Change to smaller size hook.

Rnd 2: Do **not** turn; work Picot, slip st in next sc, (work Picot, slip st in next 3 sc) 32 times, work Picot, slip st in next sc, (work Picot, slip st in next 3 sc) 14 times, work Picot, slip st in next sc, (work Picot, slip st in next 3 sc) 19 times, work Picot, slip st in next sc, (work Picot, slip st in next 3 sc) 13 times, work Picot, slip st in last 2 sc; join with slip st to first slip st, finish off.

SLEEVE

Row 1: With **right** side facing, using largest size hook for Sport Weight yarn and working in Back Loops Only, join yarn with sc in st at bottom of either armhole ***(see Joining With Sc, page 26)***; sc in each sc across: 37 sc.
Rows 2-27: Ch 1, turn; sc in Back Loops Only of each sc across.
Finish off.

Sew sleeve seam.

Edging: With **right** side facing, join yarn with slip st in first sc; ch 3, slip st in second ch from hook, slip st in next 3 sc, (work Picot, slip st in next 3 sc) around; join with slip st to first slip st, finish off.

Repeat for remaining Sleeve.

Using photo as a guide, sew one 18" (45.5 cm) length of ribbon to each corner of Yoke.

BONNET

Work in Back Loops Only throughout Body ***(Fig. 3, page 27)***.

BODY

With medium size hook, ch 48.
Row 1 (Right side)**:** Sc in second ch from hook and in each ch across: 47 sc.

Note: Loop a short piece of yarn around any stitch to mark Row 1 as **right** side.

Rows 2 and 3: Ch 1, turn; sc in each sc across.
Row 4: Ch 3 ***(counts as first dc)***, turn; work Cross St across ***(Fig. 1, page 2)***: 47 dc.
Row 5: Ch 1, turn, sc in each dc across.
Rows 6-21: Repeat Rows 2-5, 4 times.
Finish off.
Fold piece in half with **wrong** side together. Matching sts, whipstitch Row 21 together for back of Bonnet ***(Fig. 6, page 27)***.

FINISHING

NECKBAND

Row 1: With **right** side facing, smaller size hook and working in ends of rows across Body, join yarn with sc in first row; work 45 sc evenly spaced across: 46 sc.
Rows 2 and 3: Ch 1, turn; sc in each sc across.
Row 4: Ch 1, turn; sc in first 10 sc, decrease, (sc in next sc, decrease) 8 times, sc in last 10 sc: 37 sc.
Row 5: Ch 1, turn; sc in each sc across; do **not** finish off.

FACEBAND

Row 1: Ch 1, do **not** turn; sc in first 4 rows; skip next row, working in free loops of beginning ch ***(Fig. 2, page 27)***, work 49 sc evenly spaced across; skip next row, sc in last 4 rows: 57 sc.
Row 2: Turn; slip st in first 3 sc, (work Picot, slip st in next 3 sc) across; finish off.

Using photo as a guide, sew one 18" (45.5 cm) length of ribbon to each corner of Bonnet.

Instructions continued on page 6.

BOOTIE (Make 2)

SQUARE

Work in Back Loops Only throughout Square ***(Fig. 3, page 27)***.

Using meduim size hook, ch 20.

Row 1 (Right side)**:** Sc in second ch from hook and in each ch across: 19 sc.

Note: Loop a short piece of yarn around any stitch to mark Row 1 as **right** side.

Rows 2 and 3: Ch 1, turn; sc in each sc across.
Row 4: Ch 3 ***(counts as first dc)***, turn; work Cross St across ***(Fig. 1, page 2)***: 19 dc.
Row 5: Ch 1, turn; sc in each dc across.
Rows 6-16: Repeat Rows 2-5 twice, then repeat Rows 2-4 once **more**.
Finish off.

INSTEP

With **right** side facing, fold Square with Row 16 and beginning ch together. Working in free loops of beginning ch ***(Fig. 2, page 27)***, whipstitch first 10 sts and first 10 chs together ***(Fig. 6, page 27)***.

TOE

Flatten piece with Instep seam centered; to close toe, sew end of rows together on same end as Instep seam.

HEEL

Fold Bootie with Instep seam at top; sew end of rows together on opposite side to close heel, leave remaining 18 sts unworked.

CUFF

Rnd 1: With **right** side facing, largest size hook for Sport Weight yarn, and working in both loops, join yarn with sc in seam at heel ***(see Joining with Sc, page 26)***; work 23 sc evenly spaced around; join with slip st to first sc: 24 sc.
Rnd 2 (Eyelet rnd)**:** Ch 4 ***(counts as first dc plus ch 1)***, ★ skip next sc, dc in next sc, ch 1; repeat from ★ around; join with slip st to first dc: 12 dc and 12 chs.
Rnd 3: Ch 1, sc in same st as joining and in each dc and each ch around; do **not** join or finish off: 24 sc.

Begin working in rows.

Rows 1-4: Ch 1, turn; sc in in Back Loops Only of each sc across.
Finish off.

Whipstitch Cuff seam.

Weave one 18" (45.5 cm) length of ribbon through Eyelet round.

AFGHAN

Note 1: Each row is worked across length of Afghan holding 2 strands of yarn together throughout.

Note 2: Work in Back Loops Only ***(Fig. 3, page 27)***, unless otherwise instructed.

With largest size hook and 2 strands of Medium Weight yarn, ch 118.

Row 1 (Wrong side)**:** Sc in second ch from hook and in each ch across: 117 sc.

Note: Loop a short piece of yarn around **back** of any stitch on Row 1 to mark **right** side.

Rows 2 and 3: Ch 1, turn; sc in each sc across.
Row 4: Ch 3 ***(counts as first dc)***, turn; work Cross St across ***(Fig. 1, page 2)***: 117 dc.
Row 5: Ch 1, turn; sc in each dc across.
Rows 6-79: Repeat Rows 2-5, 18 times; then repeat Rows 2 and 3 once **more**, do **not** finish off.

EDGING

Rnd 1: Ch 1, turn; working in both loops, 3 sc in first sc, sc in each sc across to last sc, 3 sc in last sc, work 76 sc evenly spaced across end of rows, working in free loops of beginning ch ***(Fig. 2, page 27)***, 3 sc in first ch, sc in each ch across to last ch, 3 sc in last ch, work 76 sc evenly spaced across end of rows; join with slip st to first sc: 394 sc.
Rnd 2: Do **not** turn; work Picot, skip first sc, slip st in next sc, ★ (work Picot, slip st in next 3 sc) across to center sc of next 3-sc group, work Picot, slip st in center sc; repeat from ★ around to last 2 sc, slip st in last 2 sc; join with slip st to first slip st, finish off.

Hot Pink Layette

Shown on back cover.

INTERMEDIATE

Finished Size: 6 months
Chest Measurement: 17" (43 cm)
Finished Chest Measurement: 22" (56 cm)
Afghan: 36" x 43" (91.5 cm x 109 cm)

MATERIALS

Sacque, Bonnet and Booties

LIGHT 3

Sport Weight Yarn

Complete Set

Hot Pink - 675 yards (617 meters)

Sacque

Hot Pink - 500 yards (457 meters)

Bonnet

Hot Pink - 100 yards (91 meters)

Booties

Hot Pink - 75 yards (68.5 meters)

Crochet hooks, sizes F (3.75 mm), G (4 mm) **and** H (5 mm) **or** sizes needed for gauge

3/8" (10 mm) wide Ribbon - 2 yards (2 meters)

5/8" (16 mm) Buttons - 3

Sewing needle and thread

Yarn Needle

Afghan

MEDIUM 4

Medium Weight Yarn

[4 ounces, 242 yards (113 grams, 221 meters) per skein]:

Variegated - 9 skeins

Crochet hook, size K (6.5 mm) **or** size needed for gauge

GAUGES:

Sport Weight Yarn: 17 sc and 20 rows = 4" (10 cm)
Medium Weight Yarn (holding 2 strands of yarn together)**:** 15 sc = 5 1/2" (14 cm);
Rows 1-11 of Afghan = 5" (12.75 cm)

GAUGE SWATCHES:

Sport Weight Yarn: 4" (10 cm) square

Using medium size hook and Hot Pink, ch 18.
Row 1: Sc in second ch from hook and in each ch across: 17 sc.
Rows 2-20: Ch 1, turn; sc in each sc across.
Finish off.

Medium Weight Yarn: 4 1/4" x 5" (10.75 cm x 12.75 cm)
Note: Swatch is worked holding 2 strands of yarn together.

Using largest size hook and Variegated, ch 14.
Row 1: Sc in second ch from hook, ★ ch 1, skip next 2 chs, work Shell in next ch, ch 1, skip next 2 chs, sc in next ch; repeat from ★ once **more**: 2 Shells.
Row 2: Ch 6 ***(counts as first dc plus ch 3)***, turn; sc in center dc of next Shell, ch 3, dc in next sc, ch 3, sc in center dc of next Shell, ch 3, dc in last sc: 3 dc, 2 sc and 4 ch-3 sps.
Row 3: Ch 1, turn; sc in first dc, (2 sc in next ch-3 sp, sc in next st) 4 times: 13 sc.
Row 4: Ch 1, turn; sc in each sc across.
Row 5: Ch 1, turn; sc in first sc, ★ ch 1, skip next 2 sc, work Shell in next sc, ch 1, skip next 2 sc, sc in next sc; repeat from ★ once **more**.
Rows 6-11: Repeat Rows 2-5 once; then repeat Rows 2 and 3 once **more**.
Finish off.

STITCH GUIDE

SHELL
(Dc, ch 1, dc, ch 1, dc) in st indicated.

BEGINNING SC DECREASE (uses first 2 sts)
Pull up a loop in first 2 stitches, YO and draw through all 3 loops on hook ***(counts as first sc)***.

SC DECREASE (uses next 2 sts)
Pull up a loop in next 2 stitches, YO and draw through all 3 loops on hook ***(counts as one sc)***.

SACQUE

YOKE

With Hot Pink and medium size hook, ch 64.

Row 1 (Right side)**:** Sc in second ch from hook and in each ch across: 63 sc.

Note: Loop a short piece of yarn around any stitch to mark Row 1 as **right** side.

Row 2: Ch 1, turn; sc in first 9 sc, (sc, ch 1, sc) in next sc, sc in next 11 sc, (sc, ch 1, sc) in next sc, sc in next 19 sc, (sc, ch 1, sc) in next sc, sc in next 11 sc, (sc, ch 1, sc) in next sc, sc in last 9 sc: 67 sc and 4 ch-1 sps.

Row 3: Ch 1, turn; sc in first 10 sc, (sc, ch 1, sc) in first ch-1 sp, sc in next 13 sc, (sc, ch 1, sc) in next ch-1 sp, sc in next 21 sc, (sc, ch 1, sc) in next ch-1 sp, sc in next 13 sc, (sc, ch 1, sc) in next ch-1 sp, sc in last 10 sc: 75 sc and 4 ch-1 sps.

Row 4: Ch 1, turn; sc in first 11 sc, (sc, ch 1, sc) in first ch-1 sp, sc in next 15 sc, (sc, ch 1, sc) in next ch-1 sp, sc in next 23 sc, (sc, ch 1, sc) in next ch-1 sp, sc in next 15 sc, (sc, ch 1, sc) in next ch-1 sp, sc in last 11 sc: 83 sc and 4 ch-1 sps.

Row 5: Ch 1, turn; sc in first 12 sc, (sc, ch 1, sc) in first ch-1 sp, sc in next 17 sc, (sc, ch 1, sc) in next ch-1 sp, sc in next 25 sc, (sc, ch 1, sc) in next ch-1 sp, sc in next 17 sc, (sc, ch 1, sc) in next ch-1 sp, sc in last 12 sc: 91 sc and 4 ch-1 sps.

Row 6: Ch 1, turn; sc in first 13 sc, (sc, ch 1, sc) in first ch-1 sp, sc in next 19 sc, (sc, ch 1, sc) in next ch-1 sp, sc in next 27 sc, (sc, ch 1, sc) in next ch-1 sp, sc in next 19 sc, (sc, ch 1, sc) in next ch-1 sp, sc in last 13 sc: 99 sc and 4 ch-1 sps.

Row 7: Ch 1, turn; sc in first 14 sc, (sc, ch 1, sc) in first ch-1 sp, sc in next 21 sc, (sc, ch 1, sc) in next ch-1 sp, sc in next 29 sc, (sc, ch 1, sc) in next ch-1 sp, sc in next 21 sc, (sc, ch 1, sc) in next ch-1 sp, sc in last 14 sc: 107 sc and 4 ch-1 sps.

Row 8: Ch 1, turn; sc in first 15 sc, (sc, ch 1, sc) in first ch-1 sp, sc in next 23 sc, (sc , ch 1, sc) in next ch-1 sp, sc in next 31 sc, (sc, ch 1, sc) in next ch-1 sp, sc in next 23 sc, (sc, ch 1, sc) in next ch-1 sp, sc in last 15 sc: 115 sc and 4 ch-1 sps.

Row 9: Ch 1, turn; sc in first 16 sc, (sc, ch 1, sc) in first ch-1 sp, sc in next 25 sc, (sc, ch 1, sc) in next ch-1 sp, sc in next 33 sc, (sc, ch 1, sc) in next ch-1 sp, sc in next 25 sc, (sc, ch 1, sc) in next ch-1 sp, sc in last 16 sc: 123 sc and 4 ch-1 sps.

Row 10: Ch 1, turn; sc in first 17 sc, (sc, ch 1, sc) in first ch-1 sp, sc in next 27 sc, (sc, ch 1, sc) in next ch-1 sp, sc in next 35 sc, (sc, ch 1, sc) in next ch-1 sp, sc in next 27 sc, (sc, ch 1, sc) in next ch-1 sp, sc in last 17 sc: 131 sc and 4 ch-1 sps.

Row 11: Ch 1, turn; sc in first 18 sc, (sc, ch 1, sc) in first ch-1 sp, sc in next 29 sc, (sc, ch 1, sc) in next ch-1 sp, sc in next 37 sc, (sc, ch 1, sc) in next ch-1 sp, sc in next 29 sc, (sc, ch 1, sc) in next ch-1 sp, sc in last 18 sc: 139 sc and 4 ch-1 sps.

Row 12: Ch 1, turn; sc in first 19 sc, (sc, ch 1, sc) in first ch-1 sp, sc in next 31 sc, (sc, ch 1, sc) in next ch-1 sp, sc in next 39 sc, (sc, ch 1, sc) in next ch-1 sp, sc in next 31 sc, (sc, ch 1, sc) in next ch-1 sp, sc in last 19 sc: 147 sc and 4 ch-1 sps.

Row 13: Ch 1, turn; sc in first 20 sc, (sc, ch 1, sc) in first ch-1 sp, sc in next 33 sc, (sc, ch 1, sc) in next ch-1 sp, sc in next 41 sc, (sc, ch 1, sc) in next ch-1 sp, sc in next 33 sc, (sc, ch 1, sc) in next ch-1 sp, sc in last 20 sc: 155 sc and 4 ch-1 sps.

Row 14: Ch 1, turn; sc in first 21 sc, (sc, ch 1, sc) in first ch-1 sp, sc in next 35 sc, (sc, ch 1, sc) in next ch-1 sp, sc in next 43 sc, (sc, ch 1, sc) in next ch-1 sp, sc in next 35 sc, (sc, ch 1, sc) in next ch-1 sp, sc in last 21 sc; do **not** finish off: 163 sc and 4 ch-1 sps.

Note: Place markers around 59th sc and 141st sc for Sleeve placement.

Instructions continued on page 10.

BODY

Row 1: Ch 1, turn; sc in first sc, ch 1, skip next sc, work Shell in next sc, ch 1, skip next sc, † sc in next sc, ch 1, skip next 2 sc, work Shell in next sc, ch 1, skip next 2 sc †; repeat from † to † 2 times **more**, sc in next ch-1 sp, ch 1, skip next 37 sc (Sleeve), work Shell in next ch-1 sp, ch 1, skip next sc, repeat from † to † 7 times, sc in next sc, ch 1, skip next sc, work Shell in next ch-1 sp, ch 1, skip next 37 sc (Sleeve), sc in next ch-1 sp, ch 1, skip next 2 sc, work Shell in next sc, ch 1, skip next 2 sc, repeat from † to † twice, sc in next sc, ch 1, skip next sc, work Shell in next sc, ch 1, skip next sc, sc in last sc: 18 sc and 17 Shells.

Row 2: Ch 6 ***(counts as first dc plus ch 3, now and throughout)***, turn; sc in center dc of next Shell, ch 3, dc in next sc, ★ ch 3, sc in center dc of next Shell, ch 3, dc in next sc; repeat from ★ across: 34 ch-3 sps, 18 dc and 17 sc.

Row 3: Ch 1, turn; sc in first dc, (2 sc in next ch-3 sp, sc in next st) across: 103 sc.

Row 4: Ch 1, turn; sc in each sc across.

Row 5: Ch 1, turn; sc in first sc, ★ ch 1, skip next 2 sc, work Shell in next sc, ch 1, skip next 2 sc, sc in next sc; repeat from ★ across.

Rows 6-22: Repeat Rows 2-5, 4 times; then repeat Row 2 once **more**, do **not** finish off.

EDGING

Change to smaller size hook.

Rnd 1: Ch 1, turn; 3 sc in first dc, 2 sc in next ch-3 sp, (sc in next st, 2 sc in next ch-3 sp) across to last dc, 3 sc in last dc; working in end of rows, work 29 sc evenly spaced across Body and 14 sc evenly spaced across Yoke, working in free loops of beginning ch ***(Fig. 2, page 27)***, 3 sc in first ch, sc in next 8 chs, skip next ch, sc in next 43 chs, skip next ch, sc in next 8 chs, 3 sc in last ch; working in end of rows, work 14 sc evenly spaced across Yoke and 29 sc evenly spaced across Body; join with slip st to first sc: 258 sc.

Rnd 2: Ch 1, turn; sc in first 29 sc, ch 1, skip next sc, (sc in next 6 sc, ch 1, skip next sc) twice, sc in next sc, 3 sc in next sc, sc in next 8 sc, skip next sc, sc in next 43 sc, skip next sc, sc in next 8 sc, 3 sc in next sc, sc in next 45 sc, 3 sc in next sc, sc in next 103 sc, 3 sc in last sc; join with slip st to first sc: 261 sc and 3 ch-1 sps (buttonholes).

Rnd 3: Ch 1, turn; sc in same st as joining, ch 3, skip next sc, (sc, ch 3, sc) in center sc, ★ (ch 3, skip next sc, sc in next sc) across to next corner 3-sc group, ch 3, skip next sc, (sc, ch 3, sc) in center sc; repeat from ★ 2 times **more**, ch 3, skip next sc, (sc in next sc, ch 3, skip next sc) across; join with slip st to first sc, finish off.

FIRST SLEEVE

Row 1: With **right** side facing and using medium size hook, join yarn with sc in marked sc ***(see Joining With Sc, page 26)***; ★ ch 1, skip next 2 sc, work Shell in next sc, ch 1, skip next 2 sc, sc in next sc; repeat from ★ 5 times **more**: 7 sc and 6 Shells.

Row 2: Ch 6, turn; sc in center dc of first Shell, ch 3, dc in next sc, ★ ch 3, sc in center dc of next Shell, ch 3, dc in next dc; repeat from ★ across: 7 dc, 6 sc and 12 ch-3 sps.

Row 3: Ch 1, turn; sc in first dc, (2 sc in next ch-3 sp, sc in next st) across: 37 sc.

Rows 4-8: Ch 1, turn; sc in each sc across.

Row 9: Ch 1, turn; sc in first sc, ★ ch 1, skip next 2 sc, work Shell in next sc, ch 1, skip next sc, sc in next sc; repeat from ★ across.

Rows 10-20: Repeat Rows 2-9 once, then repeat Rows 2-4 once **more**.

Row 21: Ch 1, turn; work beginning sc decrease, (sc in next 7 sc, sc decrease) 3 times, sc in next 6 sc, sc decrease: 32 sc.

Row 22: Ch 1, turn; sc in each sc across.

Row 23: Ch 1, turn; work beginning sc decrease, sc in next 4 sc, sc decrease, (sc in next 6 sc, sc decrease) 3 times: 27 sc.

Row 24: Ch 1, turn; sc in each sc across.

Row 25: Ch 1, turn; sc in first sc, ★ ch 3, skip next sc, sc in next sc; repeat from ★ across, finish off: 13 ch-3 sps.

SECOND SLEEVE

Work same as First Sleeve.

Sew sleeve seams.

BONNET

BODY

With medium size hook, ch 44.

Row 1 (Right side)**:** Sc in second ch from hook, ★ ch 1, skip next 2 chs, work Shell in next ch, ch 1, skip next 2 chs, sc in next ch; repeat from ★ across: 8 sc and 7 Shells.

Note: Loop a short piece of yarn around any stitch to mark Row 1 as **right** side.

Row 2: Ch 6 ***(counts as first dc plus ch 3)***, turn; sc in center dc of next Shell, ch 3, dc in next sc, ★ ch 3, sc in center dc of next Shell, ch 3, dc in next sc; repeat from ★ across: 8 dc, 7 sc and 14 ch-3 sps.
Row 3: Ch 1, turn; sc in first dc, (2 sc in next ch-3 sp, sc in next st) across: 43 sc.
Row 4: Ch 1, turn; sc in each sc across.
Row 5: Ch 1, turn; sc in first sc, ★ ch 1, skip next 2 sc, work Shell in next sc, ch 1, skip next 2 sc, sc in next sc; repeat from ★ across.
Rows 6-14: Repeat Rows 2-5 twice, then repeat Row 2 once **more**.
Finish off.

BACK

Row 1: With **right** side facing, skip first 20 sts and join yarn with sc in next sc ***(see Joining With Sc, page 26)***; (2 sc in next ch-3 sp, sc in next st) 4 times, leave remaining 20 sts unworked: 13 sc.

Change to largest size hook for Sport Weight yarn.

Rows 2-19: Ch 1, turn; sc in each sc across.
Finish off.

Sew Back to remaining sts on Body.

NECKBAND

Row 1: With **right** side facing, using medium size hook and working in end of rows across Body, join yarn with sc in first row; work 16 sc evenly spaced across to Back, sc in first sc, (sc decrease, sc in next sc) 4 times, work 17 sc evenly spaced across end of rows on Body: 42 sc.
Rows 2-4: Ch 1, turn; sc in each sc across; do **not** finish off.

EDGING

Row 1: Ch 1, do **not** turn; sc in end of first 4 rows across Neckband; working in free loops of beginning ch ***(Fig. 2, page 27)***, work 43 sc evenly spaced across; sc in end of last 4 rows on Neckband: 51 sc.
Row 2: Ch 1, turn; sc in first sc, ★ ch 3, skip next sc, sc in next sc; repeat from ★ across; finish off.

Using photo as a guide, sew one 18" (45.5 cm) length of ribbon to each corner of Bonnet.

Instructions continued on page 12.

BOOTIE (Make 2)

INSTEP

With medium size hook, ch 7.

Row 1: Sc in second ch from hook and in each ch across: 6 sc.

Rows 2-7: Ch 1, turn; sc in each sc across; do **not** finish off.

SIDES

Rnd 1 (Right side)**:** Ch 23, turn; being careful not to twist ch, join with slip st to first sc on Row 7; sc in end of each row across Instep; working in free loops of beginning ch ***(Fig. 2, page 27)***, sc in next 6 chs, sc in end of each row across Instep and in next 23 chs; do **not** join; place marker to mark beginning of rnd: 43 sc.

Bootie is now worked in continuous rounds. Place a marker at beginning of each round and do **not** join unless specified.

Note: Loop a short piece of yarn around any stitch to mark Rnd 1 as **right** side.

Rnds 2-4: Sc in each sc around; do **not** finish off.

SOLE

Rnd 1: Working in Back Loops Only ***(Fig. 3, page 27)***, sc in next 8 sc, sc decrease, sc in next 4 sc, sc decrease, sc in next 14 sc, sc decrease, sc in next 2 sc, sc decrease, sc in next 7 sc: 39 sc.

Rnd 2: Working in both loops, sc in next 8 sc, sc decrease, sc in next 2 sc, sc decrease, sc in next 14 sc, sc decrease twice, sc in next 7 sc: 35 sc.

Rnd 3: Sc in next 8 sc, sc decrease twice, sc in next 13 sc, sc decrease twice, sc in next 6 sc; slip st in next sc, finish off: 31 sc.

Whipstitch bottom of Sole together ***(Fig. 6, page 27)***.

CUFF

Rnd 1 (Eyelet rnd)**:** With **right** side facing and working in free loops of ch-23, join yarn with slip st in twelfth ch; ch 4 ***(counts as first dc plus ch 1)***, skip next ch, (dc in next ch, ch 1, skip next ch) 5 times, (dc in next sc, ch 1, skip next sc) twice, (dc in next sc, ch 1) twice, skip next ch, (dc in next ch, ch 1, skip next ch) 5 times; join with slip st to first dc: 15 dc and 15 ch-1 sps.

Rnd 2: Ch 1, sc in same st, ch 1, ★ † skip next ch and next dc, work Shell in next ch, ch 1, skip next dc and next ch †, sc in next dc, ch 1; repeat from ★ 3 times **more**, then repeat from † to † once; join with slip st to first sc: 5 sc and 5 Shells.

Rnd 3: Ch 6 ***(counts as first dc plus ch 3)***, sc in center dc of next Shell, ★ ch 3, dc in next sc, ch 3, sc in center dc of next Shell, ch 3; repeat from ★ 3 times **more**; join with slip st to first dc: 5 dc, 5 sc and 10 ch-3 sps.

Rnd 4: Ch 1, sc in same st, 2 sc in next ch-3 sp, (sc in next st, 2 sc in next ch-3 sp) around; join with slip st to first sc: 30 sc.

Rnd 5: Ch 1, sc in each sc around; join with slip st to first sc.

Rnd 6: Ch 1, sc in same st as joining, ch 3, skip next sc, ★ sc in next sc, ch 3, skip next sc; repeat from ★ around; join with slip st to first sc, finish off.

Weave one 18" (45.5 cm) length of ribbon through Eyelet round.

AFGHAN

Note: Entire Afghan is worked holding 2 strands of yarn together.

Using largest size hook, ch 92.

Row 1: Sc in second ch from hook, ★ ch 1, skip next 2 chs, work Shell in next ch, ch 1, skip next 2 chs, sc in next ch; repeat from ★ across: 15 Shells.

Row 2 (Right side)**:** Ch 6 ***(counts as first dc plus ch 3)***, turn; sc in center dc of next Shell, ch 3, dc in next sc, ★ ch 3, sc in center dc of next Shell, ch 3, dc in next sc; repeat from ★ across: 16 dc, 15 sc and 30 ch-3 sps.

Row 3: Ch 1, turn; sc in first dc, (2 sc in next ch-3 sp, sc in next st) across: 91 sc.

Row 4: Ch 1, turn; sc in each sc across.

Row 5: Ch 1, turn; sc in first sc, ★ ch 1, skip next 2 sc, work Shell in next sc, ch 1, skip next 2 sc, sc in next sc; repeat from ★ across.

Rows 6-90: Repeat Rows 2-5, 21 times; then repeat Row 2 once **more**, do **not** finish off.

EDGING

Rnd 1: Ch 1, turn; 3 sc in first dc, 2 sc in next ch-3 sp, (sc in next st, 2 sc in next ch-3 sp) across to last dc, 3 sc in last dc, work 105 sc evenly spaced across end of rows; working in free loops of beginning ch ***(Fig. 2, page 27)***, 3 sc in first ch, sc in each ch across to last ch, 3 sc in last ch; work 105 sc evenly spaced across end of rows; join with slip st to first sc: 400 sc.

Rnd 2: Ch 1, turn; sc in same st as joining and in each sc around working 3 sc in center sc of each 3-sc group; join with slip st to first sc: 408 sc.

Rnd 3: Ch 1, turn; sc in same st as joining, ch 3, skip next sc, (sc, ch 3, sc) in next sc, ★ (ch 3, skip next sc, sc in next sc) across to next corner sc, (sc, ch 3, sc) in corner sc; repeat from ★ 2 times **more**, ch 3, skip next sc, (sc in next sc, ch 3, skip next sc) across; join with slip st to first sc, finish off.

Green & Blue Layette

Shown on front cover.

INTERMEDIATE

Finished Size: 6 months
Chest Measurement: 17" (43 cm)
Finished Chest Measurement: 19" (48.5 cm)
Afghan: 33" x 48" (84 cm x 122 cm)

MATERIALS

Sacque, Bonnet, Booties

LIGHT 3

Sport Weight Yarn

Complete Set
Green - 612 yards (560 meters)
Blue - 208 yards (190 meters)

Sacque
Green - 464 yards (424 meters)
Blue - 136 yards (124 meters)

Bonnet
Green - 54 yards (49.5 meters)
Blue - 66 yards (60.5 meters)

Booties
Green - 100 yards (91 meters)
Blue - 6 yards (5.5 meters)

Crochet hooks, sizes F (3.75 mm) **and** G (4 mm) **or** sizes needed for gauge
3/8" (10 mm) wide Ribbon - 2 yards (2 meters)
5/8" (16 mm) Buttons - 3
Sewing needle and thread
Yarn needle

Afghan

MEDIUM 4

Medium Weight Yarn
[4 ounces, 242 yards (113 grams, 221 meters) per skein]:
Variegated - 6 skeins
Blue - 4 skeins
Crochet hook, size K (6.5 mm) **or** size needed for gauge

GAUGES

Sport Weight Yarn:
18 sc = 3 1/2" (9 cm); 12 rows = 2 1/2" (6.25 cm)
4 3-st groups = 3" (7.5 cm);
6 rows = 2 1/2" (6.25 cm)
Medium Weight Yarn (holding 2 strands of yarn together)**:** 4 3-st groups = 5 1/2" (14 cm);
5 rows = 3 1/2" (9 cm)

GAUGE SWATCHES

Sport Weight Yarn: 4 1/2" x 5" (11.5 cm x 12.75 cm)

Using medium size hook and Green, ch 19.
Row 1: (Tr, ch 1, sc) in fourth ch from hook, ★ skip next 2 chs, (2 tr, ch 1, sc) in next ch; repeat from ★ across: 6 3-st groups.
Row 2: Ch 2, turn; skip first sc, (2 tr, ch 1, sc) in next tr, ★ skip next tr and next sc, (2 tr, ch 1, sc) in next tr; repeat from ★ across changing to Blue in last sc made ***(Fig. 4a, page 27)***.
Row 3: Ch 2, turn; skip first sc, (2 tr, ch 1, sc) in next tr, ★ skip next tr and next sc, (2 tr, ch 1, sc) in next tr; repeat from ★ across.
Row 4: Ch 2, turn; skip first sc, (2 tr, ch 1, sc) in next tr, ★ skip next tr and next sc, (2 tr, ch 1, sc) in next tr; repeat from ★ across changing to Green in last sc made.
Row 5: Repeat Row 3.
Rows 6-12: Repeat Rows 2-5 once, then repeat Rows 2-4 once **more**.
Finish off.

Medium Weight Yarn: 4 1/8" x 4 1/4" (10.5 cm x 10.75 cm)
Note: Swatch is worked holding 2 strands of yarn together.

Using largest size hook and Variegated, ch 10.
Row 1: (Tr, ch 1, sc) in fourth ch from hook, ★ skip next 2 chs, (2 tr, ch 1, sc) in next ch; repeat from ★ once **more**: 3 3-st groups.
Rows 2-6: Work same as Sport Weight Gauge Swatch.
Finish off.

STITCH GUIDE

TREBLE CROCHET ***(abbreviated tr)***
YO twice, insert hook in stitch indicated, YO and pull up a loop (4 loops on hook), (YO and draw through 2 loops on hook) 3 times.
DECREASE (uses next 2 sts)
Pull up a loop in next 2 sts, YO and draw through all 3 loops on hook ***(counts as one sc)***.

SACQUE

SKIRT

With Green and using largest size hook for Sport Weight yarn, ch 28.
Row 1 (Right side)**:** (Tr, ch 1, sc) in fourth ch from hook, ★ skip next 2 chs, (2 tr, ch 1, sc) in next ch; repeat from ★ across: 9 3-st groups.

Note: Loop a short piece of yarn around any stitch to mark Row 1 as **right** side.

Row 2: Ch 2, turn; skip first sc, (2 tr, ch 1, sc) in next tr, ★ skip next tr and next sc, (2 tr, ch 1, sc) in next tr; repeat from ★ across changing to Blue in last sc made ***(Fig. 4a, page 27)***.
Row 3: Ch 2, turn; skip first sc, (2 tr, ch 1, sc) in next tr, ★ skip next tr and next sc, (2 tr, ch 1, sc) in next tr; repeat from ★ across.
Row 4: Ch 2, turn; skip first sc, (2 tr, ch 1, sc) in next tr, ★ skip next tr and next sc, (2 tr, ch 1, sc) in next tr; repeat from ★ across changing to Green in last sc made.
Row 5: Repeat Row 3.
Rows 6-57: Repeat Rows 2-5, 13 times.
Row 58: Repeat Row 3; finish off.

RIGHT FRONT YOKE

Row 1: With **right** side facing and working in end of rows on Skirt; join Green with sc in Row 58 ***(see Joining With Sc, page 26)***; work 22 sc evenly spaced across first 14 rows, leave remaining 44 rows unworked: 23 sc.
Rows 2-11: Ch 1, turn; 2 sc in first sc, (skip next sc, 2 sc in next sc) across to last 2 sc, skip next sc, sc in last sc.
Row 12 (Neck shaping)**:** Ch 1, turn; 2 sc in first sc, skip next sc, (2 sc in next sc, skip next sc) 6 times, sc in next sc, leave last 8 sc unworked: 15 sc.
Row 13: Ch 1, turn; 2 sc in first sc, (skip next sc, 2 sc in next sc) across to last 2 sc, skip next sc, sc in last sc.
Row 14: Ch 1, turn; 2 sc in first sc, skip next sc, (2 sc in next sc, skip next sc) 5 times, sc in next sc, skip next sc, sc in last sc: 14 sc.
Row 15: Ch 1, turn; sc in first sc, 2 sc in next sc, (skip next sc, 2 sc in next sc) across to last 2 sc, skip next sc, sc in last sc.
Row 16: Ch 1, turn; 2 sc in first sc, skip next sc, (2 sc in next sc, skip next sc) 5 times, decrease: 13 sc.
Rows 17-20: Ch 1, turn; 2 sc in first sc, (skip next sc, 2 sc in next sc) across to last 2 sc, skip next sc, sc in last sc.
Finish off.

BACK YOKE

Row 1: With **right** side facing and working in end of rows on Skirt; join Green with sc in next row from Right Front Yoke; work 50 sc evenly spaced across next 30 rows, leave remaining 14 rows unworked: 51 sc.
Rows 2-20: Ch 1, turn; 2 sc in first sc, (skip next sc, 2 sc in next sc) across to last 2 sc, skip next sc, sc in last sc.
Finish off.

LEFT FRONT YOKE

Row 1: With **wrong** side facing and working in end of rows on Skirt; join Green with sc in first row; work 22 sc evenly spaced across to Back Yoke: 23 sc.
Rows 2-20: Work same as Right Front Yoke.

Instructions continued on page 16.

With **right** side facing, whipstitch shoulder seams ***(Fig. 6, page 27)***.

FIRST SLEEVE

Row 1: With **right** side facing, using larger size hook for Sport Weight yarn and working in end of rows on Yokes, join Green with sc in st at bottom of either armhole; work 40 sc evenly spaced around: 41 sc.

Rows 2-24: Ch 1, turn; 2 sc in first sc, (skip next sc, 2 sc in next sc) across to last 2 sc, skip next sc, sc in last sc.

Row 25: Ch 1, turn; sc in first 2 sc, (skip next sc, sc in next 2 sc) across: 28 sc.

Row 26: Ch 1, turn; sc in first 4 sc, (skip next sc, sc in next 5 sc) across changing to Blue in last sc made: 24 sc.

Rows 27-29: Ch 1, turn; sc in each sc across. Finish off.

Sew sleeve seam.

Repeat for second Sleeve.

FRONT AND NECK EDGING

Row 1: With **right** side facing and using smaller size hook, join Blue with sc in first st on Row 58 of Skirt; work 27 sc evenly spaced across, work 10 sc evenly spaced across end of rows of Front Right Yoke to Neck Shaping, 3 sc in first sc, sc in next 6 sc, pull up a loop in last sc and in end of next row, YO and draw through all 3 loops on hook ***(counts as one sc)***, work 10 sc evenly spaced across end of rows to Back Yoke, sc in next 25 sc, work 10 sc evenly spaced across end of rows to last row, pull up a loop in last row and in next sc, YO and draw through all 3 loops on hook ***(counts as one sc)***, sc in next 6 sc, 3 sc in next sc, work 10 sc evenly spaced across end of rows on Left Front Yoke; working in free loops of beginning ch ***(Fig. 2, page 27)***, work 28 sc evenly spaced across: 141 sc.

Row 2: Ch 1, turn; sc in each sc around working 3 sc in center sc of each corner 3-sc group: 145 sc.

Row 3: Ch 1, turn; sc in first 28 sc, (ch 1, skip next sc, sc in next 4 sc) twice, ch 1, skip next sc, sc in next sc, 3 sc in next sc, sc in each sc across working 3 sc in next corner sc, sc in each sc across; finish off.

Sew buttons to edging opposite buttonholes.

BONNET

CROWN

With Green and using largest size hook for Sport Weight yarn, ch 43.

Row 1 (Right side)**:** (Tr, ch 1, sc) in fourth ch from hook, ★ skip next 2 chs, (2 tr, ch 1, sc) in next ch; repeat from ★ across: 14 3-st groups.

Note: Loop a short piece of yarn around any stitch to mark Row 1 as **right** side.

Row 2: Ch 2, turn; skip first sc, (2 tr, ch 1, sc) in next tr, ★ skip next tr and next sc, (2 tr, ch 1, sc) in next tr; repeat from ★ across, changing to Blue in last sc made ***(Fig. 4a, page 27)***.

Row 3: Ch 2, turn; skip first sc, (2 tr, ch 1, sc) in next tr, ★ skip next tr and next sc, (2 tr, ch 1, sc) in next tr; repeat from ★ across.

Row 4: Repeat Row 2, changing to Green in last sc made.

Row 5: Repeat Row 3.

Rows 6-8: Repeat Rows 2-4.
Finish off.

BACK

Row 1: With **right** side facing, skip first 5 3-st groups and join Green with slip st in next tr; ch 4 ***(counts as first tr)***, (tr, ch 1, sc) in same st, ★ skip next tr and next sc, (2 tr, ch 1, sc) in next tr; repeat from ★ 2 times **more**, leave remaining sts unworked: 4 3-st groups.

Rows 2-10: Repeat Rows 2-5 of Crown twice, then repeat Row 2 once **more**.
Finish off.

Sew Back to remaining sts on Body.

FACE AND NECK BANDS
Rnd 1: With **right** side facing, using smaller size hook, and working in free loops of beginning ch ***(Fig. 2, page 27)***, join Blue with sc in first ch; 2 sc in same st, sc in each ch across to last ch, 3 sc in last ch; work 14 sc evenly spaced across end of rows to Back, work 8 sc evenly spaced across Row 10 of Back, work 14 sc evenly spaced across end of rows; join with slip st to first sc: 81 sc.
Rnds 2 and 3: Ch 1, turn; sc in each sc around working 3 sc in center sc of each corner 3-sc group; join with slip st to first sc.
Finish off.

Using photo as a guide, sew one 18" (45.5 cm) length of ribbon to each corner of Bonnet.

BOOTIE (Make 2)
INSTEP
With largest size hook for Sport Weight yarn and Green, ch 7.
Row 1: Sc in second ch from hook and in each ch across: 6 sc.
Rows 2-7: Ch 1, turn; sc in each sc across; do **not** finish off.

SIDES
Rnd 1 (Right side)**:** Ch 22, turn; being careful not to twist ch, join with slip st to first sc on Row 7; sc in end of each row across Instep; working in free loops of beginning ch ***(Fig. 2, page 27)***, sc in next 6 chs, sc in end of each row across Instep and in next 22 chs; do **not** join, place marker to mark beginning of rnd: 42 sc.

Bootie is now worked in continuous rounds. Place marker after each round; do **not** join unless specified.

Note: Loop a short piece of yarn around any stitch to mark Rnd 1 as **right** side.

Rnds 2-4: Sc in each sc around; do **not** finish off.

SOLE
Rnd 1: Sc in next 7 sc, decrease, sc in next 4 sc, decrease, sc in next 14 sc, decrease, sc in next 2 sc, decrease, sc in next 7 sc: 38 sc.
Rnd 2: Sc in next 7 sc, decrease, sc in next 2 sc, decrease, sc in next 14 sc, decrease twice, sc in next 7 sc: 34 sc.
Rnd 3: Sc in next 7 sc, decrease twice, sc in next 13 sc, decrease twice, sc in next 6 sc; slip st in next sc, finish off: 30 sc.

Whipstitch bottom of Sole ***(Fig. 6, page 27)***.

CUFF
Rnd 1: With **right** side facing and working in free loops of ch-22, join Blue with sc in twelfth ch ***(see Joining With Sc, page 26)***; work 29 sc evenly spaced around; join with slip st to first sc: 30 sc.
Rnd 2 (Eyelet rnd)**:** Ch 4 ***(counts as first dc plus ch 1)***, skip next sc, ★ dc in next sc, ch 1, skip next sc; repeat from ★ around; join with slip st to first dc: 15 dc and 15 ch-1 sps.

Instructions continued on page 18.

Rnd 3: Ch 1, sc in same st as joining and in each dc and each ch-1 sp around; join with slip st to first sc, finish off.
Rnd 4: With **right** side facing, join Green with slip st in first sc; ch 4 ***(counts as first tr, now and throughout)***, (tr, ch 1, sc) in same st, skip next 2 sc, ★ (2 tr, ch 1, sc) in next sc, skip next 2 sc; repeat from ★ around; join with slip st to first tr: 10 3-st groups.
Rnd 5: Slip st in next tr, ch 4, (tr, ch 1, sc) in same st, ★ skip next sc and next tr, (2 tr, ch 1, sc) in next tr; repeat from ★ around; join with slip st to first tr, finish off.

Weave one 18" (45.5 cm) length of ribbon through Eyelet round.

AFGHAN

Note: Each row is worked across length of Afghan, holding 2 strands of yarn together throughout. When joining yarn and finishing off, leave an 8" (20.5 cm) end for fringe.

Using largest size hook and Variegated, ch 106.
Row 1 (Right side)**:** (Tr, ch 1, sc) in fourth ch from hook, ★ skip next 2 chs, (2 tr, ch 1, sc) in next ch; repeat from ★ across: 35 3-st groups.

Note: Loop a short piece of yarn around any stitch to mark Row 1 as **right** side.

Row 2: Ch 2, turn; skip first sc, (2 tr, ch 1, sc) in next tr, ★ skip next tr and next sc, (2 tr, ch 1, sc) in next tr; repeat from ★ across, finish off.
Row 3: With **right** side facing, join Blue with slip st in first sc; ch 2, (2 tr, ch 1, sc) in next tr, ★ skip next tr and next sc, (2 tr, ch 1, sc) in next tr; repeat from ★ across.
Row 4: Ch 2, turn; skip first sc, (2 tr, ch 1, sc) in next tr, ★ skip next tr and next sc, (2 tr, ch 1, sc) in next tr; repeat from ★ across, finish off.

Row 5: With **right** side facing, join Variegated with slip st in first sc; ch 2, (2 tr, ch 1, sc) in next tr, ★ skip next tr and next sc, (2 tr, ch 1, sc) in next tr; repeat from ★ across.
Rows 6-46: Repeat Rows 2-5, 10 times; then repeat Row 2 once **more**.

Holding 4 strands of both colors of yarn, each 16" (40.5 cm) long, add additional fringe to edge with yarn ends ***(Figs. 5a & b, page 27)***, then add 5 strands of both colors of yarn, each 16" (40.5 cm) long to opposite end of Afghan.

Blue & Red Layette

Shown on page 1.

INTERMEDIATE

Finished Size: 6 months
Chest Measurement: 17" (43 cm)
Finished Chest Measurement:
$23^1/_4$" (59 cm)
Afghan: $34^1/_2$" x $47^1/_2$" (87.5 cm x 120.5 cm)

MATERIALS

Sacque, Bonnet, Booties

LIGHT 3

Sport Weight Yarn

Complete Set

Blue - 981 yards (897 meters)
Red - 108 yards (99 meters)

Sacque

Blue - 675 yards (617 meters)
Red - 50 yards (45.5 meters)

Bonnet

Blue - 200 yards (183 meters)
Red - 50 yards (45.5 meters)

Booties

Blue - 106 yards (97 meters)
Red - 8 yards (7.5 meters)

Crochet hooks, sizes F (3.75 mm) **and** G (4 mm) **or** sizes needed for gauge
$^3/_8$" (10 mm) wide Ribbon - 2 yards (2 meters)
$^5/_8$" (16 mm) Buttons - 5
Sewing needle and thread
Yarn needle

Afghan

MEDIUM 4

Medium Weight Yarn [5 ounces, 302 yards (140 grams, 276 meters) per skein]:
Blue - 11 skeins
Red - 1 skein

Crochet hook, size K(6.5 mm) **or** size needed for gauge

GAUGES

Sport Weight Yarn: 4 dc = 1" (2.5 cm);
4 rows = $1^1/_4$" (3.25 cm)
Medium Weight Yarn (holding 2 strands together):
5 dc = $1^3/_4$" (4.5 cm); 3 rows = $1^1/_2$" (3.75 cm)

GAUGE SWATCHES

Sport Weight Yarn: $4^1/_4$" x $1^1/_2$"
(10.75 cm x 3.75 cm)

Using medium size hook and Sport Weight Blue, ch 19.
Row 1: Dc in fourth ch from hook ***(3 skipped chs count as first dc)*** and in each ch across: 17 dc.
Row 2: Ch 1, turn; sc in first dc, (work Puff St, sc in next 3 dc) across: 4 Puff Sts and 13 sc.
Row 3: Ch 3 ***(counts as first dc, now and throughout)***, turn; dc in each st across.
Row 4: Ch 1, turn; sc in first 3 dc, work Puff St, (sc in next 3 dc, work Puff St) across to last dc, sc in last dc: 4 Puff Sts and 13 sc.
Row 5: Ch 3, turn; dc in each st across; finish off.

Medium Weight Yarn:
6" x $2^1/_2$" (15.25 cm x 6.25 cm)
Note: Swatch is worked holding 2 strands of yarn together.

Using largest size hook and Medium Weight Blue, ch 19.
Rows 1-5: Work same as Sport Weight Gauge Swatch: 17 sts.

Instructions continued on page 20.

STITCH GUIDE

PUFF STITCH (uses one st)
YO, insert hook in next st, YO and pull up a loop, YO and draw through 2 loops on hook, ★ YO, insert hook in **same** st, YO and pull up a loop, YO and draw through 2 loops on hook; repeat from ★ 2 times **more**, YO and draw through all 5 loops on hook. Push Puff St to **right** side.
BEGINNING SC DECREASE (uses first 2 sts)
Pull up a loop in first 2 sts, YO and draw through all 3 loops on hook ***(counts as one sc)***.
SC DECREASE (uses next 2 sts)
Pull up a loop in next 2 sc, YO and draw through all 3 loops on hook ***(counts as one sc)***.
BEGINNING DC DECREASE (uses first 2 sts)
Ch 2, turn; dc in next st ***(counts as one dc)***.
DC DECREASE (uses next 2 sts)
★ YO, insert hook in **next** st, YO and pull up a loop, YO and draw through 2 loops on hook; repeat from ★ once **more**, YO and draw through all 3 loops on hook ***(counts as one dc)***.

SACQUE

BODY

Body is worked in one piece to armholes.

Using medium size hook and Blue, ch 85.
Row 1 (Right side)**:** Dc in fourth ch from hook ***(3 skipped chs count as first dc)*** and in each ch across: 83 dc.

Note: Loop a short piece of yarn around any stitch to mark Row 1 as **right** side.

Row 2: Ch 1, turn; sc in first dc, work Puff St, (sc in next 3 dc, work Puff St) across to last dc, sc in last dc: 62 sc and 21 Puff Sts.
Row 3: Ch 3 ***(counts as first dc, now and throughout)***, turn; dc in each st across: 83 dc.
Row 4: Ch 1, turn; sc in first 3 dc, (work Puff St, sc in next 3 dc) across: 63 sc and 20 Puff Sts.
Row 5: Ch 3, turn; dc in next st and in each st across.
Rows 6-19: Repeat Rows 2-5, 3 times; then repeat Rows 2 and 3 once **more**, do **not** finish off.

LEFT FRONT YOKE

Row 1 (Neck shaping)**:** Ch 1, turn; work beginning sc decrease, sc in next dc, work Puff St, (sc in next 3 dc, work Puff St) 3 times, sc in next 4 dc, leave remaining 63 dc unworked: 15 sc and 4 Puff Sts.
Row 2 (Decrease row)**:** Ch 3, turn; dc in next st and each st across to last 2 sts, dc decrease: 18 dc.
Row 3: Ch 1, turn; work beginning sc decrease, sc in next dc, work Puff St, (sc in next 3 dc, work Puff St) across to last 2 dc, sc in last 2 dc: 13 sc and 4 Puff Sts.
Row 4: Repeat Row 2: 16 dc.
Row 5: Ch 1, turn; work beginning sc decrease, sc in next dc, work Puff St, (sc in next 3 dc, work Puff St) twice, sc in last 4 dc: 3 Puff Sts and 12 sc.
Row 6: Repeat Row 2: 14 dc.
Row 7: Ch 1, turn; sc in first 3 dc, (work Puff St, sc in next 3 dc) twice, work Puff St, sc in last 2 dc: 11 sc and 3 Puff Sts.
Row 8: Repeat Row 2: 13 dc.

Row 9: Ch 1, turn; sc in first 4 dc, work Puff St, sc in next 3 dc, work Puff St, sc in last 4 dc: 11 sc and 2 Puff Sts.
Row 10: Repeat Row 2: 12 dc.
Row 11: Ch 1, turn; sc in first dc, work Puff St, (sc in next 3 dc, work Puff St) twice, sc in last 2 dc: 9 sc and 3 Puff Sts.
Row 12: Repeat Row 2: 11 dc.
Row 13: Ch 1, turn; sc in first 2 dc, work Puff St, sc in next 3 dc, work Puff St, sc in last 4 dc; finish off: 9 sc and 2 Puff Sts.

BACK
Row 1: With **wrong** side facing, join Blue with sc in first unworked dc from Row 1 of Left Front Yoke ***(see Joining With Sc, page 26)***; sc in next 2 dc, (work Puff St, sc in next 3 dc) 10 times, leave remaining 20 dc unworked: 33 sc and 10 Puff Sts.
Row 2: Ch 3, turn; dc in next st and in each st across: 43 dc.
Row 3: Ch 1, turn; sc in first dc, work Puff St, (sc in next 3 dc, work Puff St) across to last dc, sc in last dc: 32 sc and 11 Puff Sts.
Row 4: Ch 3, turn; dc in next st and in each st across: 43 dc.
Row 5: Ch 1, turn; sc in first 3 dc, (work Puff St, sc in next 3 dc) across: 33 sc and 10 Puff Sts.
Rows 6-13: Repeat Rows 2-5 twice.
Finish off.

RIGHT FRONT YOKE
Row 1: With **wrong** side facing, join Blue with sc in first unworked dc from Row 1 of Back; sc in next 3 dc, work Puff St, (sc in next 3 dc, work Puff St) across to last 3 dc, sc in next dc, sc decrease: 15 sc and 4 Puff Sts.
Row 2 (Decrease row)**:** Work beginning dc decrease, dc in next st and in each st across: 18 dc.
Row 3: Ch 1, turn; sc in first 2 dc, work Puff St, (sc in next 3 dc, work Puff St) across to last 3 dc, sc in next dc, sc decrease: 13 sc and 4 Puff Sts.
Row 4: Repeat Row 2: 16 dc.
Row 5: Ch 1, turn; sc in first 4 dc, work Puff St, (sc in next 3 dc, work Puff St) twice, sc in next dc, sc decrease: 12 sc and 3 Puff Sts.
Row 6: Repeat Row 2: 14 dc.
Row 7: Ch 1, turn; sc in first 2 dc, (work Puff St, sc in next 3 dc) across: 11 sc and 3 Puff Sts.
Row 8: Repeat Row 2: 13 dc.
Row 9: Ch 1, turn; sc in first 4 dc, work Puff St, sc in next 3 dc, work Puff St, sc in last 4 dc: 11 sc and 2 Puff Sts.
Row 10: Repeat Row 2: 12 dc.
Row 11: Ch 1, turn; sc in first 2 dc, work Puff St, (sc in next 3 dc, work Puff St) twice, sc in last dc: 9 sc and 3 Puff Sts.
Row 12: Repeat Row 2: 11 dc.
Row 13: Ch 1, turn; sc in first 4 dc, work Puff St, sc in next 3 dc, work Puff St, sc in last 2 dc; finish off: 9 sc and 2 Puff Sts.

Whipstitch shoulder seams ***(Fig. 6, page 27)***.

SLEEVES
Row 1: With **right** side facing, join Blue with slip st in same st as last st worked on Row 1 of Back; ch 3, work 32 dc evenly spaced around armhole edge: 33 dc.
Row 2: Ch 1, turn; sc in first dc, (work Puff St, sc in next 3 dc) across: 25 sc and 8 Puff Sts.
Row 3: Ch 3, turn; dc in next st and in each st across.
Row 4: Ch 1, turn; sc in first 3 dc, work Puff St, (sc in next 3 dc, work Puff St) across to last dc, sc in last dc: 25 sc and 8 Puff Sts.
Row 5: Repeat Row 3.
Rows 6-15: Repeat Rows 2-5 twice; then repeat Rows 2 and 3 once **more**.
Row 16 (Cuff)**:** Ch 1, turn; sc in first dc, (sc decrease, sc in next dc) across to last 2 dc, sc decrease: 22 sc.
Row 17: Ch 1, turn; sc in each sc across changing to Red in last sc made ***(Fig. 4a, page 27)***.
Row 18: Ch 1, turn, sc in each sc across.
Row 19: Ch 1, turn; sc in each sc across changing to Blue in last sc made.
Rows 20 and 21: Ch 1, turn, sc in each sc across.
Finish off.

Repeat for second Sleeve.

Sew sleeve seams.

Instructions continued on page 22.

EDGING

Rnd 1: With **right** side facing, using medium size hook and working in free loops of beginning ch ***(Fig. 2, page 27)***, join Blue with sc in center ch; sc in next 40 chs, 3 sc in last ch; work 25 sc evenly spaced across end of rows to neck shaping, 3 sc in first row, work 19 sc evenly spaced across to Back; sc in next 21 sts, work 19 sc evenly spaced across end of rows on neck shaping, 3 sc in last row, work 25 sc evenly spaced across; working in free loops of beginning ch, 3 sc in first ch, sc in next 40 chs; join with slip st to first sc: 202 sc.
Rnd 2: Ch 1, turn; sc in same st as joining and in each sc around, working 3 sc in center sc of each corner, changing to Red in last sc made; join with slip st to first sc: 210 sc.
Rnd 3: Ch 1, turn; sc in same st as joining and in each sc around, working 3 sc in center sc of each corner; join with slip st to first sc: 218 sc.
Rnd 4 (Buttonhole)**:** Ch 1, turn; sc in same st as joining and in each sc across to center sc of next corner, 3 sc in center sc, sc in next 2 sc, (ch 1, skip next sc, sc in next 6 sc) 4 times, ch 1, skip next sc, 3 sc in center sc, sc in each sc around, working 3 sc in center sc of each remaining corner, changing to Blue in last sc made; join with slip st to first sc: 221 sc and 5 ch-1 sps (buttonholes).
Rnd 5: Ch 1, turn; sc in same st as joining and in each sc and each ch-1 sp around, working 3 sc in center sc of each corner; join with slip st to first sc; finish off: 234 sc.

Sew buttons to edging opposite buttonholes.

BONNET

CROWN

With Blue and using medium size hook, ch 47.
Row 1 (Right side)**:** Dc in fourth ch from hook ***(3 skipped chs count as first dc)*** and in each ch across: 45 dc.

Note: Loop a short piece of yarn around any stitch to mark Row 1 as **right** side.

Row 2: Ch 1, turn; sc in first 3 dc, work Puff St, (sc in next 3 dc, work Puff St) across to last dc, sc in last dc: 34 sc and 11 Puff Sts.
Row 3: Ch 3 ***(counts as first dc, now and throughout)***, turn; dc in next st and in each st across.
Row 4: Ch 1, turn; sc in first dc, (work Puff St, sc in next 3 dc) across: 34 sc and 11 Puff Sts.
Row 5: Ch 3, turn; dc in next st and in each st across.
Rows 6-12: Repeat Rows 2-5 once, then repeat Rows 2-4 once **more**.
Finish off.

BACK

Row 1: With **right** side facing, skip first 15 sts and join Blue with slip st in next sc; ch 3, dc in next 14 sts, leave remaining 15 sts unworked: 15 dc.

Row 2: Ch 1, turn; sc in first dc, work Puff St, (sc in next 3 dc, work Puff St) across to last dc, sc in last dc: 11 sc and 4 Puff Sts.

Row 3: Ch 3, turn; dc in next st and in each st across.

Row 4: Ch 1, turn; sc in first 3 dc, (sc in next 3 dc, work Puff St) across: 12 sc and 3 Puff Sts.

Row 5: Ch 3, turn; dc in next st and in each st across.

Rows 6-11: Repeat Rows 2-5 once, then repeat Rows 2 and 3 once **more**.

Finish off.

Sew Back to remaining sts on Crown.

BRIM

Row 1: With **right** side facing, using smaller size hook, and working in free loops of beginning ch ***(Fig. 2, page 27)***; skip first 13 chs and join Blue with sc in next ch ***(see Joining With Sc, page 26)***; sc in next 18 chs, leave remaining 13 chs unworked: 19 sc.

Rows 2-4: Ch 1, turn; work beginning sc decrease, sc in each sc across to last 2 sc, sc decrease: 13 sc.

Finish off.

EDGING

Rnd 1: With **right** side facing and using smaller size hook, join Blue with slip st to center dc of Back; ch 1, pull up a loop in same st and in next dc, YO and draw through all 3 loops on hook ***(counts as first sc)***, sc decrease 3 times, working in end of rows on Crown, work 16 sc evenly spaced across; working in free loops of beginning ch, 3 sc in first ch, sc in next 12 chs, sc in end of next 3 rows on Brim, 2 sc in next sc, sc in next 11 sc, 2 sc in last sc, skip first row, sc in end of next 3 rows; working in free loops of beginning ch, sc in next 12 chs, 3 sc in last ch; work 16 sc evenly spaced across end of rows on Crown; sc decrease 3 times, pull up a loop in last dc and in same st as first sc made, drop Blue, with Red ***(Fig. 4b, page 27)***, YO and draw through all 3 loops on hook ***(counts as one sc)***; join with slip st to first sc: 91 sc.

Rnd 2: Ch 1, sc in same st and in next 20 sc, 3 sc in next sc, sc in next 12 sc, skip next sc, sc in next 3 sc, 2 sc in next sc, sc in next 13 sc, 2 sc in next sc, sc in next 3 sc, skip next sc, sc in next 12 sc, 3 sc in next sc, sc in next 21 sc; join with slip st to first sc: 95 sc.

Rnd 3: Ch 1, turn; sc in first 7 sc, (sc decrease, sc in next 3 sc) 3 times, 3 sc in next sc, sc in next 12 sc, skip next sc, sc in next 3 sc, 2 sc in next sc, sc in next 15 sc, 2 sc in next sc, sc in next 3 sc, skip next sc, sc in next 12 sc, 3 sc in next sc, (sc in next 3 sc, sc decrease) 3 times, sc in next 7 sc changing to Blue in last sc made; join with slip st to first sc: 93 sc.

Rnd 4: Ch 1, turn; sc in first 20 sc, 3 sc in next sc, sc in next 12 sc, skip next sc, sc in next 3 sc, 2 sc in next sc, sc in next 17 sc, 2 sc in next sc, sc in next 3 sc, skip next sc, sc in next 12 sc, 3 sc in next sc, sc in next 20 sc; join with slip st to first sc, finish off: 94 sc.

Using photo as a guide, sew one 18" (45.5 cm) length of ribbon to each corner of Bonnet.

Instructions continued on page 24.

BOOTIE (Make 2)

INSTEP

Using medium size hook, and Blue, ch 8.

Row 1: Dc in fourth ch from hook ***(3 skipped chs count as first dc)*** and in each ch across: 6 dc.

Rows 2-4: Ch 3 ***(counts as first dc, now and throughout)***, turn; dc in next dc and in each dc across; do **not** finish off.

SIDES

Rnd 1 (Right side)**:** Ch 22, turn; being careful not to twist ch, join with slip st to first sc on Row 4; ch 3, work 6 dc evenly spaced across end of rows on Instep; working in free loops of beginning ch ***(Fig. 2, page 27)***, dc in each ch across, work 7 dc evenly spaced across end of rows on Instep, dc in each ch around; do **not** join, place marker to mark beginning of rnd: 42 dc.

Sides and Sole are worked in continuous rounds. Place a marker after each round and do **not** join unless specified.

Note: Loop a short piece of yarn around any stitch to mark Rnd 1 as **right** side.

Rnd 2: Dc in each dc around; do **not** finish off.

SOLE

Rnd 1: Working in Back Loops Only ***(Fig. 3, page 27)***, sc in next 7 dc, sc decrease, sc in next 4 dc, sc decrease, sc in next 14 dc, sc decrease, sc in next 2 dc, sc decrease, sc in next 7 dc: 38 sc.

Rnd 2: Working in both loops, sc in next 7 sc, sc decrease, sc in next 2 sc, sc decrease, sc in next 14 sc, sc decrease twice, sc in next 7 sc: 34 sc.

Rnd 3: Sc in next 7 sc, sc decrease twice, sc in next 13 sc, sc decrease twice, sc in next 6 sc: 30 sc.

Rnd 4: Sc in next 7 sc, sc decrease, sc in next 13 sc, sc decrease, sc in next 6 sc; slip st in next sc, finish off: 28 sc.

Whipstitch bottom of Sole ***(Fig. 6, page 27)***.

CUFF

Rnd 1: With **right** side facing and working in free loops of ch-22, join Blue with slip st in twelfth ch; ch 3, work 30 dc evenly spaced around; join with slip st to first dc: 31 dc.

Begin working in rows.

Row 1: Ch 1, turn; sc in same st as joining, work Puff St, (sc in next 3 dc, work Puff St) across to last dc, sc in last dc: 23 sc and 8 Puff Sts.

Row 2: Ch 3, turn; dc in next st and in each st across.

Row 3: Ch 1, turn, sc in first 3 dc, (work Puff St, sc in next 3 dc) across: 24 sc and 7 Puff Sts.

Row 4: Ch 1, turn; sc in each st across changing to Red in last sc made ***(Fig. 4a, page 27)***.

Row 5: Ch 1, turn; sc in each sc across.

Row 6: Repeat Row 4, changing to Blue in last sc made.

Row 7: Ch 1, turn; sc in each sc across; finish off.

Sew Cuff seam.

Weave one 18" (45.5 cm) length of ribbon through dc on Rnd 1 of Cuff.

AFGHAN

Note: Entire Afghan is worked holding 2 strands of yarn together throughout.

With Blue and using larger size hook, ch 89.

Row 1 (Right side): Dc in fourth ch from hook ***(3 skipped chs count as first dc)*** and in each ch across: 87 dc.

Note: Loop a short piece of yarn around any stitch to mark Row 1 as **right** side.

Row 2: Ch 1, turn; sc in first dc, work Puff St, (sc in next 3 dc, work Puff St) across to last dc, sc in last dc: 65 sc and 22 Puff Sts.

Row 3: Ch 3 ***(counts as first dc, now and throughout)***, turn; dc in next st and in each st across: 87 dc.

Row 4: Ch 1, turn; sc in first 3 dc, (work Puff St, sc in next 3 dc) across: 66 sc and 21 Puff Sts.

Row 5: Ch 3, turn; dc in next st and in each st across.

Rows 6-87: Repeat Rows 2-5, 20 times; then repeat Rows 2 and 3 once **more**, do **not** finish off.

EDGING

Rnd 1: Ch 1, turn; 3 sc in first dc, sc in each dc across to last dc, 3 sc in last dc, sc evenly across end of rows; working in free loops of beginning ch ***(Fig. 2, page 27)***, 3 sc in first ch, sc in each ch across to last ch, 3 sc in last ch; sc evenly spaced across end of rows; join with slip st to first sc.

Rnd 2: Ch 1, turn; sc in each sc around working 3 sc in center sc of each 3-sc group, changing to Red in last sc made ***(Fig. 4b, page 27)***; join with slip st to first sc.

Rnd 3: Ch 1, turn; sc in each sc around working 3 sc in center sc of each 3-sc group; join with slip st to first sc.

Rnd 4: Ch 1, turn; sc in each sc around working 3 sc in center sc of each 3-sc group, changing to Blue in last sc made; join with slip st to first sc.

Rnds 5 and 6: Ch 1, turn; sc in each sc around working 3 sc in center sc of each 3-sc group; join with slip st to first sc.

Finish off.

GENERAL INSTRUCTIONS

ABBREVIATIONS

ch(s)	chain(s)
cm	centimeters
dc	double crochet(s)
tr	treble crochet(s)
mm	millimeters
Rnd(s)	Round(s)
sc	single crochet(s)
sp(s)	space(s)
st(s)	stitch(es)
YO	yarn over

★ — work instructions following ★ as many **more** times as indicated in addition to the first time.

† to † — work all instructions from first † to second † **as many** times as specified.

( ) or [ ] — work enclosed instructions **as many** times as specified by the number immediately following **or** work all enclosed instructions in the stitch or space indicated **or** contains explanatory remarks.

colon (:) — the number(s) given after a colon at the end of a row or round denote(s) the number of stitches or spaces you should have on that row or round.

GAUGE

Exact gauge is **essential** for proper size and fit. Before beginning your project, make the sample swatch given in the individual instructions in the yarn and hook specified. After completing the swatch, measure it, counting your stitches and rows or rounds carefully. If your swatch is larger or smaller than specified, **make another, changing hook size to get the correct gauge**. Keep trying until you find the size hook that will give you the specified gauge.

JOINING WITH SC

When instructed to join with sc, begin with a slip knot on hook. Insert hook in stitch or space indicated, YO and pull up a loop, YO and draw through both loops on hook.

Yarn Weight Symbol & Names	SUPER FINE 1	FINE 2	LIGHT 3	MEDIUM 4	BULKY 5	SUPER BULKY 6
Type of Yarns in Category	Sock, Fingering Baby	Sport, Baby	DK, Light Worsted	Worsted, Afghan, Aran	Chunky, Craft, Rug	Bulky, Roving
Crochet Gauge Ranges in Single Crochet to 4" (10 cm)	21-32 sts	16-20 sts	12-17 sts	11-14 sts	8-11 sts	5-9 sts
Advised Hook Size Range	B-1 to E-4	E-4 to 7	7 to 1.9	I-9 to K-10.5	K-10.5 to M-13	M-13 and Larger

CROCHET TERMINOLOGY		
UNITED STATES		**INTERNATIONAL**
slip stitch (slip st)	=	single crochet (sc)
single crochet (sc)	=	double crochet (dc)
half double crochet (hdc)	=	half treble crochet (htr)
double crochet (dc)	=	treble crochet (tr)
treble crochet (tr)	=	double treble crochet (dtr)
double treble crochet (dtr)	=	triple treble crochet (ttr)
triple treble crochet (tr tr)	=	quadruple treble crochet (qtr)
skip	=	miss

CROCHET HOOKS													
U.S.	B-1	C-2	D-3	E-4	F-5	G-6	H-8	I-9	J-10	K-10½	N	P	Q
Metric - mm	2.25	2.75	3.25	3.5	3.75	4	5	5.5	6	6.5	9	10	15

BEGINNER	Projects for first-time crocheters using basic stitches. Minimal shaping.
EASY	Projects using yarn with basic stitches, repetitive stitch patterns, simple color changes, and simple shaping and finishing.
INTERMEDIATE	Projects using a variety of techniques, such as basic lace patterns or color patterns or color patterns, mid-level shaping and finishing.
EXPERIENCED	Projects with intricate stitch patterns, techniques and dimension, such as non-repeating patterns, multi-color techniques, fine threads, small hooks, detailed shaping and refined finishing.

FREE LOOPS OF A CHAIN

When instructed to work in a free loop of a beginning chain, work in loop indicated by arrow *(Fig. 2)*.

Fig. 2

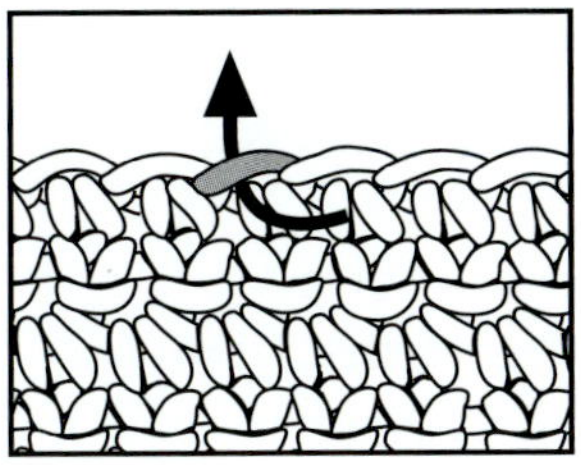

BACK OR FRONT LOOP ONLY

Work only in loop(s) indicated by arrow *(Fig. 3)*.

Fig. 3

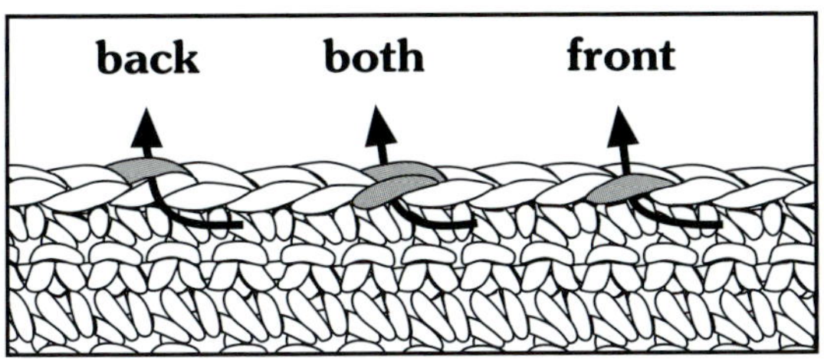

CHANGING COLORS

Work the last stitch to within one step of completion, hook new yarn *(Figs. 4a or b)* and draw through all loops on hook. Cut old yarn and work over both ends, unless otherwise specified.

Fig. 4a

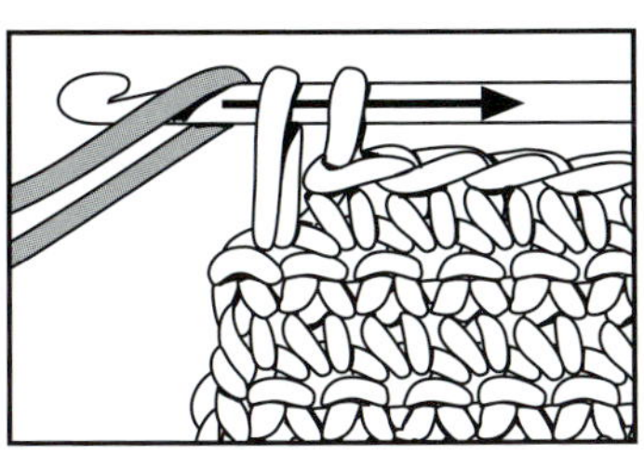

Fig. 4b

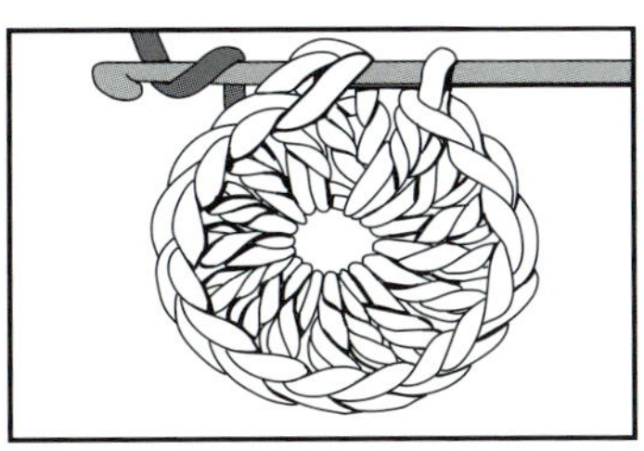

FRINGE

Cut a piece of cardboard 5" (12.5 cm) wide and 8" (20.5 cm) long. Wind the yarn **loosely** and **evenly** lengthwise around the cardboard until the card is filled, then cut across one end; repeat as needed. Hold together as many strands as specified in individual instructions; fold in half.

With **wrong** side facing and using a crochet hook, draw the folded end up through a row and pull the loose ends through the folded end *(Fig. 5a)*; draw the knot up **tightly** *(Fig. 5b)*. Repeat, spacing as desired. Lay flat on a hard surface and trim the ends.

Fig. 5a

Fig. 5b

WHIPSTITCH

Place two pieces with **wrong** sides together. Sew through both pieces once to secure the beginning of the seam, leaving an ample yarn end to weave in later. Insert the needle from **front** to **back** through **both** loops on **both** pieces *(Fig. 6)*. Bring the needle around and insert it from **front** to **back** through next loops of both pieces. Continue in this manner across, keeping the sewing yarn fairly loose.

Fig. 6

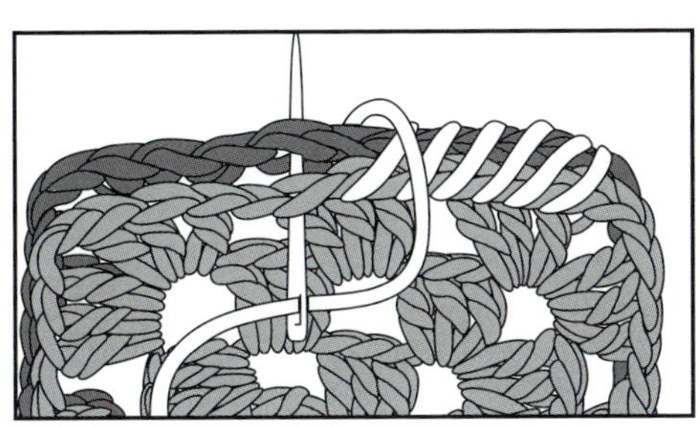

YARN INFORMATION

All garments in this leaflet were made with Sport Weight Yarn.
All afghans were made with Medium Weight Yarn.
Any brand in the specified weight of Yarn may be used.
It is best to refer to the yardage/meters when determining how many balls or skeins to purchase.
Remember, to arrive at the finished size, it is the GAUGE/TENSION
that is important, not the brand of yarn.

For your convenience, listed below are the specific yarns
used to create our photography models.

Purple Layette
Red Heart® Sport
#585 Purple
Red Heart® Kids
#2930 Crayon
#652 Limeade
#846 Skipper Blue

Hot Pink Layette
Red Heart® Sport
#922 Hot Pink
Red Heart® Kids
#2963 Happy

Green & Blue Layette
Red Heart® Sport
#652 Limeade
#846 Skipper Blue
Red Heart® Kids
#2845 Blue
#2940 Beach

Blue & Red Layette
Red Heart® Sport
#846 Skipper Blue
#904 Jockey Red
Red Heart® Kids
#2845 Blue
#2390 Red

We have made every effort to ensure that these instructions are accurate and complete. We cannot, however, be responsible for human error, typographical mistakes, or variations in individual work.

Production services provided by Emerald Ideas, Inc.